A Quilt of Memories Warmed by Her Hands

In patchwork colors, laughter sewn,
Her stories spin, like yarn that's grown.
Each square a tale, from old to new,
A cozy laugh, a comfort too.

She stitched our dreams, with threads of cheer,
The love she shares, we all hold dear.
A fabric of life, both soft and strong,
In her warm quilt, we all belong.

Dreams Shared Over Tea

In teacups small, ideas brew,
"Don't spill it, dear!" she gently coos.
With every sip, a giggle spreads,
"Don't forget to eat!" she softly said.

Conversations bloom, like flowers bright,
Stories dance in morning light.
Over warm mugs, plans take flight,
With mom beside, the world feels right.

The Garden Path of Good Intentions

We planted roots in rich, warm soil,
With watering cans and loving toil.
"Don't step there!" she'll yell with glee,
As flowers sway, a sight to see.

In bright sun rays, we grow and sprout,
With herb and bloom, there is no doubt.
In her little patch, joy takes reign,
Weeding worries, sharing the gain.

Cradle of Dreams Under Her Watchful Eye

With lullabies and gentle sighs,
She rocked those dreams beneath the skies.
"Dream big, my love!" she'd sing so sweet,
As stars above felt the heartbeat.

In cradled arms, we found our way,
With silly jokes to brighten the day.
Her playful watch, a guiding star,
In her embrace, we're never far.

Journeying Through Her Embrace

In the kitchen, she bakes bread,
Singing tunes, with dough on her head.
"Just add love!" she always says,
Life's a feast in so many ways.

A map of hugs, and careful chats,
With wisdom wrapped in silly hats.
Life's a dance, a silly jig,
Come join the fun, just wear a wig!

Light in Our Eyes

She says, "Laugh when things go wrong!"
With her jokes, we can't stay long.
A tickle here, a wink right there,
Her laughter floats like springtime air.

Through sunny skies and rainy days,
A spark of joy in countless ways.
She taught us all to dance through strife,
And find pure joy in this wild life.

Cuddles on Cloudy Days

When the skies turn dull and grey,
She brings hot cocoa, what a day!
With blankets and stories intertwined,
A cozy hug, so well-defined.

"Keep smiling now!" she laughs, so bright,
Turning gloom into sheer delight.
With a sprinkle of warmth and cheer,
The world is perfect when she's near!

The Melody of Her Heartstring

With pots and pans, she makes her sounds,
Each clatter brings joy that astounds.
Dancing wildly in our small space,
She leads the way with love's embrace.

Her silly songs, a twinkling bell,
In each verse, there's a tale to tell.
Life's a chorus, fun and loud,
In her warmth, we feel so proud!

Scribbled Notes on the Fridge Door

Eat your greens, or so she swore, \ Might just help you soar. \ Socks in the dryer, where'd they go? \ Just like life's secrets, they ebb and flow. \ \ Dance like no one is keeping score, \ Laundry piles like a mountain's core. \ Laugh 'til your stomach starts to ache, \ It's the joy that makes you awake. \ \ Count the crumbs, share your snack, \ Wisdom is always in the back. \ Find the missing tees and never pout, \ That's what life is all about.

Embraces That Hold the World

Hugs that feel like a cozy quilt, \ Make the worries seem to wilt. \ Hands to guide you when you're lost, \ She'll remind you, it's worth the cost. \ \ Ice cream fixes all that's broken, \ I'll share her secrets, unspoken. \ Laughter dances in the air, \ Turns a frown into a dare. \ \ With each squeeze, a world's unfold, \ Her love's a story, bright and bold. \ Just remember, it's not all serious, \ Life's a joke, so be delirious.

Recipes for Happiness

A dash of laughter, pinch of time, \ Stir in love, it's always prime. \ Boil the dreams, don't let them burn, \ Life's a recipe, it's your turn. \ \ Whisk away doubts, sprinkle some joy, \ Each ingredient, pure as a toy. \ Serve with grace, a smile on the side, \ Happiness dwells in what's supplied. \ \ Remember to share, and double the fun, \ Even mistakes can lead to a pun. \ Taste the moments, let them blend, \ In each bite, a love that won't end.

Echoes of Comfort in Her Voice

Her laughter floats like a sweet refrain, \ Chasing away all the mundane pain. \ Tucking in dreams as daylight fades, \ She whispers stories like playful parades. \ \ "Eat your cake, and don't you fret!" \ Those words are hugs you won't forget. \ "Life's not perfect, and that's okay!" \ With each echo, worries sway. \ \ Recipes shared for storms and strife, \ A melody sweet, the song of life. \ Her voice is magic, a charm so bright, \ Guiding us gently through day and night.

Reflections in Her Silhouette

In the kitchen, she stirs her brew,
Counting each sip like it's a clue.
"Life's a dance," she boldly claims,
"Best done in mismatched socks and games."

With a wink, she hands me toast,
"Burnt? Just a meal that loves you most!"
Life's a circus, she insists with glee,
"Laugh a lot; it's the best recipe!"

Paper Flowers and Eternal Joys

She crafts with scissors, paper bright,
"You'll never see the world in white!"
Each flower blooms with giggles loud,
"Make mistakes, my little cloud."

In her garden, weeds are dreams,
Even chaos, she gently redeems.
"Life's a party, wear your best hat,
And bring your goofy dance with that!"

The Secret Language of Hand-Held Hearts

In her purse, there's wisdom to find,
Biscuit crumbs and dreams entwined.
"Feelings are hugs wrapped in a laugh,"
She says, as she counts a new giraffe.

With her hand, she paints the air,
"Life's a canvas, show you care!"
Secrets whispered with a grin,
"Take two cookies; you'll always win!"

Solace in Her Unspoken Words

Her eyes twinkle like stars at night,
"When in trouble, make it light!"
She says the quiet carries tunes,
Sung by the softest, cuddly moons.

Her smiles hold stories, ever broad,
"Life's a puzzle; don't go hard!"
A nudge and a laugh, her gentle sway,
"Always find joy—in every day!"

Garden of Dreams, Nurtured with Care

In her garden, tall weeds sway,
"Just like dreams, they won't obey!"
Planting hopes in rows so neat,
Watering wishes, oh so sweet.

She talks to flowers, they bloom bright,
"Listen, dear, they'll share their light!"
With petals soft, and colors bold,
Secrets of life just waiting to be told.

Don't fear the bugs, they're just like us,
Finding snacks in the summer's fuss.
Sprinkle laughter, plant a smile,
Your dreams will grow, just give them a while.

With sunlight's kiss and gentle rain,
She finds joy in every strain.
In her garden, life's playful schemes,
Flourish deep in our wildest dreams.

The Softest Touch in Times of Trouble

When storms roll in and moments clash,
Mom's soft words come in a flash.
"Grab a cookie, it's quite the heal,
Life's too short to miss the feel!"

She's got a potion, brewed with care,
Laughter and hugs floating in the air.
With chocolate chips and a wink so sly,
Every problem just seems to fly.

In tough times, she'll sit real close,
"This too shall pass, let's raise a toast!"
With cozy blankets and silly talks,
Worries drift like old worn socks.

So when life throws its wildest game,
Just remember, you're not to blame.
With a sprinkle of love and a dash of cheer,
Mom's softest touch will always be near.

Songs Sung in Morning Light

In the morning, sunbeams tease,
Mom's singing flows through gentle breeze.
"Get up, sleepyhead! Join the fun,
Life's a song waiting to be spun!"

She shakes the curtains, dances around,
With pots and pans, she makes a sound.
"Stir the oatmeal, don't let it burn!
Life's an adventure! Take your turn!"

With every note, the day begins,
Laughter erupts, chasing off sins.
"It's pancakes today, so take a slice,
With syrup drizzles, oh so nice!"

In her songs, wisdom's hidden tight,
Joyful echoes from morning light.
With each sweet lyric, life takes flight,
In our hearts, she's always bright.

Found Wisdom Beneath Thin Walls

Beneath the roof, whispers flow,
Mom's quirky truths steal the show.
"Life's like laundry, full of spins,
Sometimes you lose, sometimes you win!"

She giggles softly, all tucked in,
Hiding secrets where stories begin.
"Beneath thin walls, humor thrives,
In echoes of laughter, love survives."

With borrowed shoes, she'll spin a tale,
"Wear your mom's heels, and never fail!"
In her world of socks and dreams,
Wisdom flows in hilarious streams.

So lean in close, hear her call,
In the chaos, there's joy for all.
Mom's got nuggets, all wrapped with cheer,
Beneath thin walls, her voice is clear.

Echoes of Her Voice

In every little giggle, she finds the gold,
With stories retold, never getting old.
'Watch out for puddles!' she shouts with glee,
As I splash around, feeling wild and free.

Life's a comedy, wrapped in her hugs,
We laugh at the fluff of her dog's fuzzy bugs.
'Just dance like no one's watching,' she claims,
While I trip on my feet and forget all names.

She serves wisdom in cookies and tea,
'Add a pinch of joy for the best jubilee!'
Through all of life's chaos, she holds my hand,
With her giggles and warmth, I truly understand.

Her laughter, like music, fills up the air,
Reminding me sweetly that life's truly rare.
In her playful banter, I find my way,
With every soft whisper, she brightens my day.

Candles in the Dark

When nights feel eerie, and shadows grow long,
She lights her candles, singing a song.
'Fear not the whispers that dance on the wall,'
With a wink and a smile, she conquers it all.

She says, 'Life's like cake, with layers to taste,'
And slathers on frosting, no moment to waste.
'When life gives you lemons, don't just make pie,'
Add sugar and sprinkles, we'll aim for the sky!

With a flashlight in hand, she leads the way,
Finding lost treasures and games we can play.
In her world of giggles, it's all just a lark,
With candles aglow, we dance in the dark.

So when troubles loom heavy, and frowns start to form,
Remember her laughter, like a sweet summer storm.
For in every dark moment, a spark's gonna light,
With candles of joy, we'll win every fight.

Time's Gentle Teacher

She laughs at my questions, perplexed and wide,
'Time's not a river, it's a crazy ride!'
With every small wrinkle, she wears it with grace,
A map of adventures, each laugh holds a place.

'Age is just numbers; don't fret, my dear,'
As she bakes the cookies with a splash of cheer.
Her wisdom is casual, with jokes on the side,
'Conquer each birthday with cupcakes as pride!'

Though clocks keep on ticking, she dances in slow,
Embracing the moments, letting it flow.
'Take life like a puzzle, piece by piece,'
With giggles and giggles, we both find release.

So, here's to the moments, both silly and sweet,
Her playful embrace is my favorite treat.
With time as our teacher, each tick is a rhyme,
In a waltz of laughter, we conquer the climb.

A Handwritten Recipe for Happiness

Grab two cups of laughter and a pinch of play,
Mix in some cuddles to brighten the day.
Stir in a splash of mischief and fun,
Bake it with love till it's golden and done.

Add sprinkles of joy, just a dash of surprise,
A warm hug to coat it, like sweet lullabies.
Serve on a platter, invite all your friends,
With giggles and stories, the fun never ends.

If things get too sticky, don't worry, my dear,
Just sprinkle with kindness, and serve with no fear.
Life's flavored with chaos, but that's how we thrive,
Taste every adventure; it's how we arrive.

So here's my dear recipe, passed down with cheer,
From a mother to daughter, it's perfectly clear:
Happiness bubbles when you're true to yourself,
Just open your heart, there's no need for a shelf.

Sunlight through the Kitchen Window

In morning's glow, she brews her tea,
With whispers of warmth, she laughs with glee.
Dancing shadows paint the wall,
Life's great joke, she tells us all.

She stirs the pot with a knowing smile,
Says, "Chase your dreams, just walk a mile!"
Between the toast and jam's delight,
Happiness found in every bite.

Her secrets swirl in buttered bread,
"Life's a banquet!" she boldly said.
With crumbs and crumbs of humor slid,
Laughter's the spice, she always did.

At dusk, she hums her favorite tune,
And every note makes the sun swoon.
Through the window, the world is bright,
Her joke on life? It's pure insight.

Sheltering Rainbows

Rain clouds gather, then burst wide,
With laughter spilling, she takes it in stride.
"Life's a splash of color," she'll exclaim,
Like puddles that play the happiness game.

Umbrellas twirl in a whimsical dance,
"Never miss a chance to prance!"
She dons her hat, paints the sky bright,
Chasing storms with sheer delight.

Coffee's brewed strong, the warmth we crave,
Each laugh like sunshine, a moment to save.
With frothy milk and giggles in tow,
She shows us all how to steal the show.

Her rainbow whispers, a vibrant song,
Through life's puddles, we all belong.
With a wink and a grin, she flings wide the door,
Joy's umbrella shelters us, forevermore.

A Symphony of Heartbeats

A waltz of chaos fills the air,
She conducts our lives with loving flair.
"Tap your feet to your own beat!"
"Life's a series of funny tweets!"

With silly stories, she tunes our souls,
Each heartbeat thumping, laughter rolls.
Pots and pans clang like symphonic bliss,
In her kitchen, there's harmony, not a miss.

Swaying through the mess, she finds the rhyme,
With chocolate chip cookies, well worth the time.
"Add a dash of joy, a pinch of cheer,
Every note's a memory to hold dear!"

Through life's concert, we dance and play,
Orchestrated moments, come what may.
In this delightful, bustling show,
Her funny tune is the sweetest flow.

Faces of Love

A smile like sunshine, her magic's clear,
With goofy faces, she brings us cheer.
Through winks and nods, we share a plot,
"Life is a sketch, give it all you've got!"

In every frown, she'll find a grin,
With silly faces, we all dive in.
"Play the fool, laugh till you ache!"
With hugs so tight, there's no mistake.

Her voice, a melody, soft and sweet,
Warmed by laughter, life feels complete.
Through tears and joy, she paints our days,
With funny faces, she leads the way.

When shadows loom, she shows the light,
Her heart full of humor, brilliant and bright.
With every giggle and every shove,
We find our truth in the faces of love.

Whispers of Wisdom In the Kitchen

In the kitchen, she hums a tune,
Spills the secrets—flour and gloom.
"A pinch of salt, but not too much!"
Laughter rises, her gentle touch.

She stirs the pot with a witty grin,
"Life's like soup, it's better with skin!"
Chopping onions, she blinks and sighs,
"Crying's okay, but laugh till you cry!"

Cookie baking, the oven's hot,
"Life's sweet—just don't burn the pot!"
With every bite, she beams so bright,
"Make the most of each silly bite!"

In every sprinkle, in every mess,
"Find joy in chaos, nothing less!"
Muffins rise, and so do dreams,
"Add some giggles, or so it seems!"

Threads of Love in Every Stitch

With needles clicking, she spins her tale,
"Life's like knitting, never stale!"
"Drop a stitch? Just call it art!"
Every fabric holds a loving heart.

She ties a knot, with a wink so sly,
"Sometimes things unravel, oh me, oh my!"
"But don't you fret, just take a chance,
Stitch your moments as you dance!"

A patch for every scrap of thought,
"In the world's quilt, it's love I sought!"
"Colorful patches make us whole,
Sew tight those dreams, they warm the soul!"

And when she finishes—what a sight!
"Each thread's a laugh, each snag's alright!"
Wear your stories, let them glow,
"In this fabric of fun, let love flow!"

Nighttime Stories Under Starry Skies

Under stars, with cozy beds,
She weaves tales through sleepy heads.
"Once upon a time, with a dragon bold,
Life's an adventure, or so we're told!"

The glow of night wraps us tight,
"Even monsters can be polite!"
"Chase your dreams, don't be shy,
Just keep your slippers nearby!"

Her laughter dances with the moon,
"Every ending's a chance for a tune!"
"So sprinkle giggles and chase the fears,
With each tale told, let joy adhere!"

Under blankets, time slips away,
"Sleep is a journey, come what may!"
She whispers softly, stories unfurl,
"Life's a book—go on, give it a whirl!"

Lessons in Laughter by the Hearth

By the hearth, the flames do crack,
She pours hot cocoa, gives a smack!
"Life's like chocolate, bittersweet,
But add some sugar, and it's a treat!"

With each marshmallow, giggles ignite,
"Laughter's the spark that feels so right!"
She quips and smiles, with warmth abound,
"Take silly selfies, dance around!"

Each witty jest is a precious gem,
"In this wild world, just be your stem!"
"For flowers bloom through joy and jest,
Find your fun, it's truly the best!"

As her stories wrap us snug,
"Happiness is a big warm hug!"
So gather 'round, let laughter lead,
In this grand comedy, plant a seed!

The Symphony of Sacrifice

In the kitchen, pots do dance,
Spaghetti sauce, a messy chance.
"Eat your greens!" she sings with glee,
While hiding chocolate, so slyly.

A symphony of chores in sight,
"Do your homework, it's only right!"
Yet when I trip, she rolls her eyes,
"Oops! Who knew? You're quite the prize!"

Each dirty dish, she claims a song,
With every fight, we can't go wrong.
"You'll thank me later, don't you stress!"
Her nagging? Oh, it's just the best!

Between the laughs and endless care,
I know she's always going to share.
In this grand symphony, we find,
Life's playful notes, humor entwined.

Footprints on the Path

Little shoes left trails of joy,
"Don't step in mud!" my mom's big ploy.
Yet every splash brings laughter loud,
She's right behind, a playful crowd.

Each tiny footprint tells a tale,
Of racing hearts that never fail.
"Look both ways!" she'd often shout,
As I would dodge and twist about.

Through every stumble, every fall,
She'd laugh and cheer, and through it all.
"You'll grow up strong, just wait and see!"
Each step with love, she'd guarantee.

With giggles shared along the way,
Those footprints lead to brighter days.
A path of joy, a winding track,
Together always, never lack.

Crumbs of Happiness

Cookie crumbs upon her dress,
"Sweet treats make life a fun mess!"
She bakes with love, and sometimes chaos,
While I'm the one who tries to play boss.

"Just one more slice!" I'd loudly plead,
As frosting drips in perfect seed.
"Just remember, share with your friends,
Or you'll face the wrath! This never ends!"

Chocolate chips and sugar high,
Each bite like laughter in the sky.
No need for fancy things or strife,
Just crumbs of joy, that's the sweet life!

Then comes the cleanup, oh what a flair,
"Baking's fun till we have to care!"
Yet through it all, I know it's true,
Those crumbs of happiness came from you.

Timeless Echoes of Laughter

From bedtime tales that never cease,
Her chuckles weave a warm fleece.
"You'll grow up quickly! Don't you dare!"
Yet time flies by, a fast affair.

In every joke, a memory made,
As sound echoes, no need to trade.
"What's your excuse for that big mess?"
Her teasing smile, I must confess.

We dance through days of silly fun,
Life's race is on, but we have won.
With giggles loud, and echoes bright,
Each cherished moment feels just right.

So here's to laughter, cheers and cheer,
My mother's voice, forever near.
In timeless echoes, we unite,
With joy that shines, a pure delight.

Adventures in a Cozy Living Room

In the corner, dust bunnies roam,
While Mom's slippers claim their home.
The couch a ship on seas of socks,
With tales of pirates and curious clocks.

Grandpa's chair rocks like a boat,
As everyone laughs, trying to gloat.
Mom tells stories, her eyes aglow,
Of adventures in gardens where wildflowers grow.

The cat, a captain, surveys the scene,
While we dream of lands that we've never seen.
Cookies baking in the warm, sweet air,
Life's little joys are found everywhere.

With every laugh, the clock ticks slow,
In our fort of pillows, we steal the show.
We search for treasures in lost, old socks,
In this cozy living room, we've built our docks.

Acts of Kindness from Memory Lane

Mom's baked goods, a warm embrace,
Each cookie holds a loving trace.
A smile wrapped in chocolate delight,
Making even Mondays feel just right.

She shares her wisdom on life's quick stroll,
Like knowing pizza is a balanced goal.
With every hug, she mends the rift,
In her eyes, all my worries drift.

She waves goodbye with her legendary cheer,
Reminding me that home is always near.
Her laughter echoes in every old hall,
Turning small moments into a grand ball.

With a wink and a nudge, she teaches me flair,
How to shine bright without any despair.
These acts of kindness, stitched in time,
Make life a dance, a joyful rhyme.

Crumbs of Comfort from the Table

At our table, crumbs are gold,
With stories shared, the heart unfolds.
Spilled milk, laughter, an epic fail,
Each bite a treasure, each tale a trail.

The mashed potatoes, a cloud so light,
As we argue who's wrong, who's right.
With every fork, a family fight,
But love is the prize, shining so bright.

Dessert's the crown, the grand finale,
With Mom in the kitchen, a joyful rally.
Pies that sing of summer sun,
In every taste, we're all just one.

The table's a canvas, smeared with glee,
Where crumbs of comfort set our hearts free.
Life's messy, yes, but we sit so fine,
Together forever, in our little dine.

Kaleidoscope of Love in Simple Moments

In a garden, we pick dandelions bright,
Dancing in sunshine, hearts take flight.
Mom shows the magic in weeds and roots,
Turning a patch into fanciful suits.

With crayons and paper, we draw our day,
Mountains of laundry become a play.
A picnic blanket for a lunch of dreams,
With juice boxes, laughter, and sunny beams.

Riding bikes with wobbly glee,
Mom shouts, 'You're a natural! Can't you see?'
A kaleidoscope brightens each little guess,
In simple moments, we find our success.

With each shared glance, the world's anew,
In the simplest ways, love shines through.
Life's whimsical spin, a beautiful jest,
In our cozy realm, we are truly blessed.

Fireflies in Twilight

In the warm glow of fading light,
Fireflies dance, oh what a sight.
My mom says, with a twinkling grin,
Life's little joys, that's where to begin.

Chasing shadows, we laugh and play,
She tells me to seize the day.
With a jar in hand, we catch the glow,
Her wise words fly, like fireflies in tow.

Every flicker, a whispered jest,
She claims happiness is the ultimate quest.
In simple things, the magic is found,
With laughter and light, we're spellbound.

So we run through fields, no care in sight,
Holding onto moments, hearts feeling light.
For in twilight glow, she makes it clear,
Joy and love are reason enough to cheer.

Healing Hands, Healing Heart

With a gentle touch and a knowing smile,
Mom fixes woes, even just for a while.
Her hands weave magic, like a soothing balm,
In her warmth, the world's troubles calm.

She says, 'Dear child, don't take life too serious,
Find fun in chaos, it's all a bit curious.'
With cookies and hugs, she mends every tear,
Making each moment an affair so rare.

So when I'm lost, feeling quite absurd,
She serves up laughter, my favorite word.
In her healing embrace, worries depart,
Mom's laughter dances, healing my heart.

Each chuckle's a bandage, a silly fix,
Her joyfulness always in the mix.
With her by my side, life's troubles grow small,
In her laughter's echo, I find it all.

The Legacy of Laughter

Mom's laughter fills the empty room,
Chasing away the shadows of gloom.
She says jokes are like sunshine beams,
Lighting our lives with the silliest dreams.

With every pun and every quip,
Her giggles twirl, a joyous trip.
A legacy built on laughter and fun,
In her light-hearted ways, we've already won.

From baked goods that flop to puns that fall flat,
She claims it's the laughter that matters, just that!
In her garden of humor, love blooms bright,
Each chuckle a flower in sheer delight.

So we stumble through life, with sides aching tight,
Her humor a treasure, a pure delight.
In every chuckle, her spirit flows free,
A legacy of laughter, oh can't you see?

Roots of Resilience

With roots so deep, they sturdy hold,
Mom teaches strength, with stories bold.
She says, 'Life's a riddle, a tricky game,
But laughter's the key, you'll never be the same.'

Through trials and tears, her smile won't fade,
She spins tales of courage, fearfully made.
In the garden of laughter, we plant our dreams,
Her humor a balm, bursting at the seams.

When storms brew strong and the skies turn gray,
Mom's quirky tales chase the clouds away.
With every giggle, resilience takes flight,
Her laughter a beacon, our guiding light.

So here's to the roots that never give in,
A testament to joy that grows from within.
In the wild woods of life, she shows me the way,
Our hearts intertwined, forever we'll play.

Beacons of Hope

When life gives you lemons, make a pie,
But don't forget to aim for the sky!
Dance like no one cares, be a little absurd,
For laughter's the lightest, sweetest word.

In every misstep, there's a chance to smile,
Like making mistakes with a flair and style.
Wear mismatched socks, don't worry or fret,
Life's a colorful game, let's not forget!

Pick dandelions, blow dreams in the air,
Each puff a wish that takes you somewhere!
Find joy in the chaos, embrace the mess,
In this zany ride, consider it a bless!

So burst out in giggles, let your heart sing,
In the dance of the crazy, you'll find the zing.
Find hope in the laughter, the fun that we share,
In each goofy moment, shows just how we care.

The Scent of Her Laugh

Her laughter, a perfume, sweet and bright,
It fills the room, makes everything right.
Like cookies fresh-baked, warm from the oven,
You know life's delightful when joy is a token.

She sprinkles her giggles like confetti in air,
Turns every dull day into a fun fair.
With a wink and a nod, she's a tricky delight,
Her puns make you snort—what a joyful sight!

A chuckle escapes like bubbles afloat,
Her joy's contagious, it makes me emote.
Life's far too short to be stoic and grim,
With her laughter, the world's full of whim.

So let the melody dance with the light,
Her laughter, my compass, guiding me right.
In a world full of rush, she's a playful breeze,
Reminding me softly—just breathe and be pleased.

Classroom of Kindness

In the school of life, love writes the rules,
Where kindness is gold and we're all silly fools.
With hugs for the heart and smiles on the face,
We learn that each moment is a warm embrace.

Forget the grades in the piles of stress,
The laughter and joy are what we assess.
Share your crayons, sing songs full of cheer,
In this classroom of kindness, shed every fear.

A lesson in giggles, we write on the wall,
For friendships and joy are the greatest of all.
So toss that textbook, let smiles be the guide,
Class is in session—let love be our pride!

So gather 'round friends, let's party and play,
In this classroom of kindness, come what may.
With hearts full of laughter and hands full of grace,
We'll learn to light up the dullest of space.

Scribbles in the Margins

Doodles and scribbles, oh what a sight,
In the margins of life, we scribble our light.
With stick figures dancing and hearts all around,
Our stories unfold without making a sound.

The pages we write, a chaotic ballet,
Mixing colors of joy in a carefree display.
With ink blots of laughter and stars that are bright,
These scribbles remind us of pure delight.

In sticky-note wisdom and coffee-stained dreams,
We sketch out our lives, bursting at the seams.
A scribble here, a doodle there,
In the grand book of living, we all have a flair!

So cherish the scribbles, the jokes that you share,
Each line a reminder that life's meant to care.
With playful inscriptions that paint our road,
In this wacky adventure, let love be our code!

The Canvas of Time Together

In crayon hues, she paints my days,
With laughter, mess, and silly ways.
Each moment's colored, bold and bright,
Her art of love is pure delight.

She says the best is yet to come,
But she can't find her favorite cup!
With every brushstroke, joy appears,
Her canvas fills with all our years.

Her Playlist of Dreams

With every tune, she sings aloud,
She dances free, forever proud.
In every note, she weaves a spell,
Her playlist rings, it's pure, it's swell.

Each song's a tale of life's own quirks,
Like when she laughed at how I lurked.
Her greatest hits break all the rules,
A chorus filled with family fools.

The Journey Between Generations

From her wise words, I gained a clue,
She's got the tales that always brew.
In every giggle and every sigh,
Her stories soar, they never die.

Through wrinkled hands, she shares her past,
With every chuckle, time goes fast.
With wisdom wrapped in humor's cloak,
She teaches love through every joke.

The Architecture of Affection

She builds our home with hugs and cheers,
Each brick a smile that disappears.
Her laughter echoes off the walls,
With each sweet story, joy enthralls.

With blueprints drawn from heart and laugh,
She crafts a life, our happy path.
Each room a lesson, cozy and sweet,
Her design makes every day complete.

Morning Coffee and Evening Stars

In the dawn, with coffee brewed,
She smiles wide, says, "Life's a mood!"
"Add some cream, a dash of bliss,
Don't forget the morning kiss!"

At night she gazes, stars aglow,
"Each one's a wink for you to know,
Life's a joke, laugh from your heart,
Like the way I burn the tart!"

Her wisdom flows like bitter brew,
"Just sip life slow, don't rush on through,
Even spilled beans can taste so sweet,
Just mop it up, life's still a treat!"

With each coffee sip, a giggle shared,
Messy life? She's unprepared!
But in the chaos, love persists,
Even if her toast's a twist!

Comfort in Chaos

Waking up in dishes piled,
She says, "Oh dear, but don't be riled!"
"It's just a sign we lived today,
Grab a broom and dance, hooray!"

When socks mismatch and time runs thin,
She winks and says, "Where to begin?"
"Life's a circus on a spree,
Just grab a stool and sit by me!"

Amidst the chaos, giggles flow,
"Life's a puzzle we can't quite know!"
"But gather 'round, my little sprites,
We'll make it rhyme on tough nights!"

With laughter loud and hugs galore,
She teaches us to seek and soar.
For in the mess, she sees the charm,
And wraps us up with loving arms!

Life Lessons from Her Embrace

In her arms, the world feels right,
She whispers, "Darling, hold on tight!"
"Life's a dance, you may just trip,
But that's the way we learn to skip!"

With each embrace, a lesson hides,
"It's okay to fall, 'cause fun abides!"
"Just laugh it off, don't take a toll,
You'll find your way, life's a stroll!"

When worries loom like heavy clouds,
She hums sweet tunes, laughs loud and proud,
"Count your giggles, forget the frowns,
Life's a caper in silly gowns!"

As she spins tales of joy and cheer,
She teaches us to face our fear.
For with each hug, we learn to thrive,
In her embrace, we feel alive!

The Art of Letting Go

Toss the worries, let them fly!
"Life's a kite, don't let it die!"
She laughs and plays as strings unwind,
"Embrace the breeze, be free of mind!"

Holding on tightly makes you frail,
"Like that old shoe, don't make it stale!"
"Life's like pudding, let it set,
Tastes better served without regret!"

When plans go haywire and things fall flat,
She just grins and says, "How 'bout that?"
"Life's a jigsaw with missing bits,
We'll paint a picture, with all the hits!"

So here's her wisdom, wrapped in fun,
"Let go, dear child, and play till done!"
With every laugh, she lights the way,
Life's a parade — come dance and sway!

The Tapestry of Sacrifices

Mom said to mind my Ps and Qs,
Life's a mix of wins and blues.
"Eat your veggies, they'll make you spry,"
But chocolate calls, and I can't lie.

She knits with yarn of toil and care,
Each stitch a lesson, rare and spare.
"Don't skip chores, keep your room neat,"
But who can resist that tempting treat?

With every hug, she weaves the truth,
About the sprightliness of youth.
"Find your passions, have your say,"
Yet Sunday naps just melt away.

Yet laughter rings through every woe,
In her embrace, I always grow.
Lessons tucked in every chat,
With a wink, she hands me snacks.

Sunlight Streaming Through Timeless Advice

She said to shine like the morning light,
With dreams that take off, soaring high and bright.
"Be kind to others, it's a rare delight,"
But I still trip over my own feet at night.

"Wear clean socks, and don't be late,"
Her wisdom shines, and it feels like fate.
A pinch of love, a dash of care,
Yet often I'm caught in a tangled snare.

When life gets tough, and shadows loom,
"Just make a cake, and fill the room!"
A sprinkle of sugar, laughter to share,
Life's little chaos turns into flair.

So I'll keep dancing on this wobbly boat,
With Mom's wise words that keep me afloat.
Sunlight streams through her joyful sights,
Making mundane days feel so right.

Unraveled Mysteries of Everyday

She said, "Beware of socks that disappear,"
Clothes often vanish without a fear.
"Keep your secrets; they're fun to hold,"
But soon your heart will be bought and sold.

"Count your blessings and count your sheep,"
Her wisdom's boundless; barely sleep.
"When life is messy, grab a broom,"
"Then dance around; you'll clear the gloom!"

Cooking secrets locked up tight,
Her recipes spark joy, pure delight.
"Mom's still the queen of tasty tricks,"
Even if dinner turns to misfits.

So here's to life, both calm and wild,
Through laughter, chaos, every child.
In her charm, the mysteries play,
Laughing through the everyday.

Heartbeats and Homemade Remedies

"When in doubt, just hug it out,"
Mom's first aid is always about.
"Drink some soup; it's good for the soul,"
But I'm convinced brownies make me whole.

With a heart that's big and full of cheer,
Her love remedies all my fear.
"Make a list; it helps to cope,"
Yet I forget it, chasing hope.

"Watch the stars, they show the way,"
Yet the couch calls for a Netflix day.
"Baking cookies will cure the blues,"
But late-night snacks, I just can't refuse.

So here's to heartbeats and tasty treats,
Mom's homemade love never depletes.
Through all the quirks and sweet calls,
Life's a party whenever she calls.

Navigating Life's Waters

In a boat of dreams, we sail afloat,
With snacks for laughter and time to gloat.
In stormy weather, she tells a joke,
'Just steer with your heart, and let love invoke.'

She said, 'Life's like swimming, just don't lose your float,
When you belly flop, you're bound to emote!
Grab a life vest, or floaties, my dear,
Make waves of joy, and silence your fear.'

Beneath the surface, the fish all chat,
About the best way to navigate that!
Moms have the compass, just watch for the signs,
With giggles and grace, she knows how to shine.'

So here we sail, on laughter's sea,
With a mother's love, we are always free.
Remember, dear child, as you follow this quest,
It's the joy in the journey that matters the best.

Sips of Wisdom

Every morning comes with a bright hot brew,
A mug of advice, just for me and you.
'Add a pinch of humor, a dash of fun,
Life's like coffee, sweeten each run.'

She said, 'When life feels bitter or cold,
Stir it with laughter, let the joy unfold.
Make friends with the beans, let worries steep,
But never let dreams turn into sleep.'

With every sip, lessons start to flow,
Don't worry about spills; just watch out below!
A sprinkle of love can brighten your day,
And if there's a mess, it's okay—just play!'

So raise your cup high to the skies so wide,
With a smile on your face, and hope as your guide.
Each sip is a treasure, a story to share,
In the brew of existence, find laughter in care.

Soft Footfalls on Dusty Roads

In the quiet of dusk, where shadows dance,
Mom walks with me, giving life a chance.
'The road may be long, but we stick together,
With love as our patchwork, we'll brave any weather.'

'You hop, I skip, in our own little way,
Collecting the laughter that's here to stay.
Every stumble we make is just part of the fun,
With giggles and grins, until the day's done.'

Footprints in sand tell a story anew,
Mom says they're maps that lead us to you.
She stops to admire, each flower's cheer,
'It's the little things, my dear, hold them near.'

As night drapes its cloak, we dance on the road,
In our own little world, with laughter bestowed.
Each moment's a treasure, a joy to unfold,
Soft footfalls in life's dance, as adventures are told.

Her Silent Prayers

In the quiet night, with stars up above,
Mom whispers softly, a chorus of love.
Each prayer is a wish, wrapped tight in a hug,
'Take life as it comes, like a warm, cozy mug.'

She laughs at my worries, with a twinkle of grace,
'Life's not a race, just enjoy the place.
Bumps in the road are just part of the game,
Find joy in the chaos, don't fear the fame.'

Her gentle reminders are like fireflies bright,
Guiding my heart through the calm and the fright.
'In laughter, find meaning, let worries be light,
Dance under the moon, and keep dreams in sight.'

So here's to the moments, the whispers and cheer,
With a mother's love, there's nothing to fear.
Her silent prayers wrap me up in delight,
In the fabric of joy, we shine through the night.

Lessons Wrapped in Everyday Rituals

In morning light, she sips her tea,
Counting blessings, not just me.
She folds the laundry with a grin,
Says, "Life's a game, just dive in!"

She dances 'round with dusting rags,
Singing songs to the family bags.
"Don't cry over spilled milk, dear!"
Her laughter bursts, that's the cheer!

Each dish washed is a life's sweet song,
She says, "You can never go wrong!"
And in her eyes, a spark of flair,
Turns chores to joy, blooms in the air.

So here's to lessons, wrapped in fun,
A smile, a chore, a day well done!
In every task, she gifts us glee,
Life's a party, come dance with me!

The Engine of Hope in Tender Hearts.

In the backyard, she plants some seeds,
Whispers hopes with gentle deeds.
"Grow tall and strong, don't be shy,"
As bees buzz near, and clouds drift by.

A corny joke with every sprout,
"Life's just beans, let's twist and shout!"
She tends to dreams, both big and small,
With watering can, she nurtures all.

When weeds compose their sneaky plot,
She laughs and says, "Give it a shot!"
For every challenge, she's a pro,
Her laughter's light, it makes us grow.

So here's to gardens and mothers wise,
In every sprout, a new surprise.
Tender hearts with hope in charge,
Planting joy, we grow, we large!

A Whisper in the Kitchen

In the kitchen, she stirs the pot,
With a chuckle, says, "Burnt's not hot!"
A dash of spice with every chat,
"Life's a feast; just have a snack!"

She flips pancakes, they fly in air,
"Catch them quick, don't lose a flair!"
With each flip, a story told,
"Add some laughter, let it unfold!"

When cookies crumble, she just grins,
"They're still delicious, where's our wins?"
In every mess, she finds the treat,
Life's like cookie dough—oh, so sweet!

So gather 'round for laughs and cheer,
In her kitchen, joy is near.
With pots and pans, she cooks up fun,
A whisper's worth a million, hon!

Lessons in the Garden

In her garden, weeds we fight,
She says, "Don't fret, just hold on tight!"
With every flower, she shares her views,
"Life's a quilt, colorful hues!"

She tells me stories of each bright bloom,
"Every petal's burst chases the gloom!"
With laughter loud, she pulls a thorn,
"It's just a prick, you'll be reborn!"

We dig and plant, our hands get dirt,
"Life's messy, but oh, it's worth!"
She teaches patience through each grow,
"In time we'll flourish, just let it flow!"

So let's embrace the sunny rays,
In the garden, love always stays.
With each challenge, she invites the fight,
Lessons in laughter, blooming bright!

Small Hands, Big Dreams

Small hands grip at the sky,
Reaching for stars so high.
Mismatched socks, a goofy grin,
In this wild world, let the fun begin.

With crayons, they draw their fate,
A dinosaur dance, they contemplate.
Giggles blend with silly screams,
In the land of sugar-plum dreams.

Legos stacked, a kingdom tall,
In their world, they can have it all.
Chocolate puddles, messy and sweet,
In the joy of play, they find their beat.

So let them soar, let them play,
In the laughter, they'll find their way.
Through spills and thrills, life's a game,
With small hands, they'll stake their claim.

Inheritances of the Heart

In her purse, a treasure trove,
Running errands, her secret grove.
Loose change and gum, a little snack,
With each find, a memory, we unpack.

Her laughter echoes, a sweet refrain,
In the chaos of life, joy's the gain.
She says, "Dance like nobody's here,"
In her presence, we conquer our fear.

From silly songs to bedtime tales,
She wears love like a coat of scales.
With hugs and kisses, she sets the tone,
In her embrace, we've always grown.

So here's to the quirks, the love that sticks,
Inheritances of heartbeats and laughs so quick.
Through ups and downs, she paves the way,
In the garden of life, she's our bouquet.

Recipes for Joy

A pinch of laughter, a dash of fun,
In Mom's kitchen, we're never done.
Flour flies like soft snowflakes,
Mixing memories in the cakes we make.

Stir in some love, and a giggle or two,
With every bite, tastes brand new.
From kitchen disasters that made us scream,
To cookies baked with a heartfelt dream.

Sprinkles on cupcakes, a vibrant hue,
Life is sweeter when shared by two.
Through kitchen powder and icing fights,
We gather stories on starry nights.

So let's savor life with every chew,
In every recipe, there's something true.
Mom's secret ingredient? A heart so bright,
In her kitchen, we find pure delight.

Under Her Watchful Eyes

Beneath the gaze of loving care,
In her house, we've got a fair share.
A nod, a wink, a nudge on the side,
With her by our side, we laugh and ride.

Through scraped knees and the homework blues,
Her wisdom comes with a friendly muse.
She knows the art of the silly dance,
Life is better when you take a chance.

In her arms, the world feels right,
Her laughter shines like a guiding light.
With every story that she unties,
We find ourselves under her watchful eyes.

Through life's ups and the wildest downs,
She spins our frowns into joyful crowns.
In her embrace, we feel quite grand,
With her laughter, we firmly stand.

The Quilt of Family Tales

Stitched with laughter, a patchwork bright,
Each square a story, a quirky delight.
Mom's wisdom woven, it's all in the thread,
Like the time dad tried, and the cake just bled.

Family secrets, all wrapped up tight,
Unraveled at dinner, oh what a sight!
With each little tale, we chuckle and sigh,
Mom's quirky lessons, like clouds in the sky.

Building Castles in the Sand

With a bucket and spade, we'd shape our dreams,
Mom'd say, 'Life's like sand, bursting at seams.'
She'd laugh as the tide washed our castles away,
'It's just the ocean's way to make you play!'

We built high towers, with moats all around,
Mom insisted on mermaids, a treasure we found.
As waves brought them down, we'd jump and we'd shout,

'We'll build more tomorrow, that's what it's about!'

Emergency Chocolate and Other Truths

When life feels like chaos, mom has a plan,
'Grab the chocolate, you can do what you can!'
A sprinkle of sweetness, to fix every woe,
'One bite's a hug, so just let it flow!'

In the face of bad days and socks that don't match,
With ice cream for dinner, and brownies to hatch.
Mom's funny wonders, a recipe clear,
'When life hands you lemons, switch to root beer!'

The Fireside Conversations

Gathered 'round warmth, with marshmallows in hand,
Mom spinning tales of our faraway land.
'Life's a cozy fire, where you roast your fears,
Just don't forget the chocolate for cheers!'

As shadows danced playfully, stories took flight,
Mom's laughter echoed through the starry night.
With tales of the crazy, the wild and the bold,
Her quirky advice is like treasures untold.

www.ingramcontent.com/pod-product-compliance
Lightning Source LLC
Chambersburg PA
CBHW071820160426
43209CB00003B/140